LONDON

A CITY OF MANY DREAMS

The publishers wish to express
their grateful thanks to the
following for allowing photo-
graphy in the locations
mentioned:

House of Lords: By permission of
the Lord Great Chamberlain and
the Lord Chancellor.

House of Commons: By
permission of the Rt Hon
Mr Speaker, House of Commons.

Mansion House: By permission of
the Rt Hon The Lord Mayor
of London.

Guildhall: By permission of the
City of London Corporation.

Big Ben: By permission of
Mr R. MacNeil, Resident
Engineer, Palace of Westminster.

James Lock & Company Limited
(hatters): By permission of James
Lock and Company Limited.

John Lobb Limited (shoemakers):
By permission of John Lobb
Limited.

Berry Bros & Rudd Limited (wine
merchants): By permission of
Berry Bros & Rudd Limited.

First English edition published by Colour Library International Ltd.
© 1982 Illustrations and text: Colour Library International Ltd.,
    99 Park Avenue, New York, N.Y. 10016, U.S.A.
This edition is published by Crescent Books.
Distributed by Crown Publishers, Inc.
h g f e d c b a
Colour separations by FER-CROM, Barcelona, Spain.
Display and text filmsetting by ACESETTERS LTD., Richmond, Surrey, England.
Printed and bound in Barcelona, Spain by CAYFOSA and EUROBINDER.
Library of Congress Catalog Card No. 82-72455
CRESCENT BOOKS 1982

LONDON
A CITY OF MANY DREAMS

Text by Benny Green

Designed by
PHILIP CLUCAS MSIAD

Produced by
TED SMART and DAVID GIBBON

CRESCENT BOOKS
NEW YORK

London was a great lake. I knew nothing of it except that it seemed to be, in some fortunate and infinitely comforting way, benign, and so crammed with miracles that you could never tire of it. The lake stretched on and on forever and ever in all directions. You could never get to know all of it. It was too vast, and time too short, for that. Its totality would always defeat you, so the best you could aspire to was to get to know your own tiny piece and perhaps later on conduct the occasional modest reconnaissance a little further afield. An aunt of mine used to take me shopping with her every Saturday morning. One time, she paused outside a dress shop in Oxford Street and asked me whether, if she were suddenly to disappear, I could find my own way home. The suggestion that she might be about to vanish was by far the most interesting thing she had ever said to me, or was ever to say to me, and I was so fascinated by it that I answered her question in a fit of abstraction, assuring her that I knew perfectly well we were only a few minutes away from our home port. But I was not at all sure. The street signs said W.1; so we could not be so very far away, but the route was tortuous, like everything else associated with my aunt, and my familiarity with it was no more than the confused, romantic jumble you would expect from a six-year-old.

It had not taken me six years, however, to perceive that London was the centre of the world even for those who had the misfortune to live somewhere else, in other towns, other countries, other continents. One of my paternal great-uncles, it was said, had been banished in youth to Australia as a parental punishment, and I could understand that. Nobody could ever possibly *want* to leave London. In the parlour of my grandfather's house there was a green-bound book called "The Pageant of the Century," offered at specially reduced rates to readers of "The Daily Herald." I was much impressed by the presumption of its editors, who were attempting to describe the century even though the year was still only 1933. Such prescience. In the book was a sepia snapshot of Threadneedle Street; the caption read: "The financial heart of the world." I remember peering at the mystery of that photograph, scrutinising its every feature in the hope of discovering some visible manifestation of the world's heart beating there. Could it be true? Confirmation seemed to come in the form of the buffers at Kings Cross Station. Childhood was a timeless time punctuated by periodic visits

to pathetically provincial relations in Yorkshire. When you alighted at Leeds, the lines stretched on, into infinity, eternity, Scotland. But when you came home again there were the buffers, standing sentinel to assert the truth that London was where the rainbow began and ended. There was nowhere further you could go, even if you wanted to. All roads led to London? Surely not. So I conducted further investigations at St. Pancras and Euston and found my theory confirmed by more buffers.

In the beginning the heart of the world was not Threadneedle Street but the congeries of sleepy, grimy streets tucked away in the corner behind Great Portland Street and Euston Road. The skyline, composed for the most part of the warped symmetry of ancient tiles and blackened, wonky chimney-stacks, seemed unexceptional, but that was because it was the only skyline I had ever known. Outsiders sometimes found it positively bizarre. One day at Clipstone Junior Mixed, Class Four was plunged into sensation when Daisy Head, infallible executrix of our intellectual estates, questioned the claim put forward in a painting by one of the class, that one of the tenements in Cleveland Street had railings along its roof. So Class Four downed brush and palette and marched out along Cleveland Street with Daisy Head leading the way, to examine the evidence. Then we marched back again, and Daisy Head gave the painter of the penal rooftop a gold star for "Observation." She also offered a special class prize for the child who could discover why the railings were there. That was fifty years ago, the prize remains unclaimed and Daisy Head long since gone to her forefathers. But the railings endure, still puncturing a much-altered skyline.

The whole district appeared to have been packed, shortly before my arrival, with eccentrics from Central Casting. There was, for instance, Old Man Marks, proprietor of our local grocery shop, an amorphous mess of a man on whose behalf we used to write letters to the Lady Almoner of Middlesex Hospital offering to donate his body for medical research. Marks had a stomach so rampant that it preceded him into a room like the outrider to a royal procession. Had Charles Darwin ever caught a glimpse of it, the ending of "Origin of Species" would not read the way it does today. The best way of describing Marks is to call him a curious experiment in Comparative Religion, a bizarre compromise between the belly of a Buddha and the eyebrows of one of those daft demons which used to be featured so heavily in evangelical propaganda. It was those eyebrows which made him a source of wonder to all right-thinking people, to say nothing of his regular customers. For reasons best known to himself, Marks plucked his eyebrows with a view to rerouting them, and if his motives remain unknown, the theory behind them was obvious enough. To put it simply, his eyebrows grew downwards and he desired them to grow upwards. And at last, after years of plucking, Nature had arrived at a witty compromise where the eyebrows grew downwards and upwards at the same time, lending his already sleepy features a comatose effect and bestowing on their owner the power to look bored and astonished simultaneously. Try to picture a Jewish Fu Manchu.

Naturally the shop paid its way, because even if there were no delicacies you required, it was always worth popping in there just to take a look at him and the remarkable interior design of which he was so proud. Imagine for instance the vast repository for pickled cucumbers standing just inside the door. It is a cross between a water-butt and a beer barrel, and contains mysterious objects calculated to raise your saliva today and have you threshing wildly on a bed of dyspepsia tomorrow. Around the barrel's base is scattered this year's fresh sawdust, a few grains of which lie supine on the brine's still surface. Two matrons stand over the barrel's rim, peering down into the dark green waters, prodding with scientific dispassion at the oceanic murk. They chat as they select; in the background the drone of smalltalk from the other customers, with rhythmic accompaniment from the proprietor's tiny wife chopping apples and herrings on a wooden slab worn into concavity by the years. One of the matrons spears a cucumber on a long fork kindly provided by the Oxford Street Corner House without the knowledge of Messrs J. Lyons and Co. She holds up the cucumber to examine its texture and says to her companion, "So why isn't your Martin married yet? I mean, he's not bad-looking." Pause for reflection as the cucumber is deftly flicked back into the barrel and exploratory jabs made at its fellows. Then the coup de grace: "Mind you, he's not *good*-looking." Out comes the chosen cucumber, brandished triumphantly aloft, like the head of a captured bandit.

Shops like that one disappeared a generation ago, chased into bankruptcy by rising municipal rates and flattened finally by the antiseptic juggernaut of the supermarkets. In fact, none of those shops from the back streets are any longer to be seen. We had a cat's meat shop, two barber shops, a coal shop, a rag-and-bone shop, a fish-and-chip shop, a shoe-maker's, a used-tyre shop, all of them swept away by what is often laughingly defined as progress. We also had an establishment called an Oil shop, presumably because once upon a time it had specialised in oil for paraffin lamps. But its owners had one day realised that they must proliferate or die,

and by the time I was old enough to peep over their counter were stocking Reckitt's Blue, Elliman's Athletic Rub, Pear's Soap, pump adaptors, ten-inch nails, bird-seed, hammers and screwdrivers, electric light bulbs, gas brackets, wall brackets, glue, paint, tintacks, ink, screws, gum, plugs, teapots, laces, pins and needles, darning wool, cotton reels and a thousand other artefacts without which life would have been intolerable and certainly less hygienic. During the Second World War, one of my aunts, the rich, snobbish one, swept into that shop and deigned to ask for a roll of lavatory paper. Had there not been a dire shortage of that vital commodity, my aunt would never have lowered herself to set foot in so plebeian an emporium. But she did, and the assistant, who was much better mannered than she, kindly obliged. My aunt looked down at the roll of white lavatory paper as though it had just crawled out of an apple. "Haven't you any pink?" The assistant gave her a look of genuine interest and asked with impeccable politeness whether she intended papering the wall or wiping her arse with it. I always felt that a preservation order should have been slapped on that shop, or at least on that assistant, but no trace either of it, or him, or of my stuck-up aunt, now remains.

An emporium of a different kind was the one in Goochie's bedroom, on the ground floor of a house in Bolsover Street. Two doors away was the Orthopaedic Hospital, which Goochie took as an auspicious sign, because the flat feet he had acquired from wearing other people's shoes were a great trial to him. The shoes were in constant supply because Goochie was what used to be known in those days as a cobbler; he had a tiny shop, big enough for himself and one customer at a time, on the bend of Greenwell Street, a serpentine thoroughfare distinguished by the fact that my grandfather had lived in it since the world began. But the cobbler's shop was not Goochie's emporium. The real business of the day he performed in bed, and it became part of the ritual of existence to go round every Saturday morning and sit listening as my father and his brothers discussed the latest market trends with Old Goochie. I call him "old" because to my infant eye his bald head when the sun shone down on it semaphored messages of ageless antiquity; in fact, his boyish face and spry, flatfooted walk gave the game away, and looking back on it, I doubt if he was much more than thirty years old. But the thing about him I can never forget was his bowler hat, which he seemed to wear on the most incongruous occasions. He literally went to bed in it, or at least it was there, perched on his head, whenever we went to call on him on Saturday mornings to discuss the agenda for the day. I see now that the inspiration for what he called the titfer was not the dash of theatricality I took it to be, but embarrassment at the smoothness of his dome. Seeing that I was impressed, he used to make jokes about it, asking, "When does a bald man stop washing his face?," waiting until puzzlement had enveloped me and then blurting out, with genuine appreciation of his own waggishness, "When he comes to his bowler hat."

Goochie embodied an intellectual contradiction which I have encountered a hundred times in a thousand places in London life, and which I have never been able to resolve – unless the answer to the mystery is the Shavian one, that we all learn those techniques which seem necessary to our spiritual good health even though we can never learn anything else. Now Goochie was a professional gambler, that is, he dreamed of making enough money from gambling to be able to retire from cobbling for a living. In his efforts to win through he repeatedly changed roles with bewildering rapidity. One minute he was a punter, the next a bookmaker; several times in his life he was both at once, speculating the stake money of his own customers with rival bookies. And he was typical of the gambling fraternity of my childhood in that although he could not for the life of him tell you what half of three and a half was, he could work out, within a fraction of a second and to the nearest halfpenny, how much you had to come back on a shilling each-way cross-treble with a four-to-one winner, a dead-heat third at five-to-four, and a non-runner. (To be frank, there were times when it didn't matter *what* you had to come back, because the bookmaker had no intention of giving it to you.) Old Goochie used to sit up in bed on Saturday mornings, a prematurely bald gentleman-philosopher in blue-and-white striped winceyette pyjamas, like the man in the Andrews Liver Salt hoarding, or Sheffield United, and a bowler hat perched on his head, while the local horse-players gathered round to watch him computing the odds with a speed and accuracy which would so utterly have frightened the life out of Albert Einstein as to inspire him to put aside forever childish pursuits like Relativity, acquire a bowler hat and some blue-and-white striped pyjamas, and get down to the really serious side of mathematics. And yet Goochie couldn't step inside the local greengrocer's for a bag of walnuts and a pound of greengages without being turned over something terrible for his change.

Imperceptibly the slow years of childhood enlarged the scope of my awareness. If London remained a vast metropolitan lake, and the bland mirror of its surface my own ignorance, then each experience was a pebble flung into the lake, sending out ripples of enlightenment. I carried out researches on a tricycle, broadening the grasp of my geography day by day. Gradually the quadrilateral of the known world expanded to be defined by Marylebone Road, Baker Street, Oxford Street and Tottenham Court Road. Most of the pebbles were handed to me by my father, a man who, having read his Dickens, loved the town with an unqualified Rabelasian delight. One autumn morning, with the brown leaves floating on the tide, we went to see if the Tower of London was still there. It was, and so was the road which ran across Tower Bridge, and which obligingly went sailing up in the air even as we watched, as though my father had stage-managed the effect for my benefit. As it went up, he made a remark to the effect that the road to heaven is paved with bad inventions, but I didn't understand him, and am not even sure

if he did. Another time he took me to the museums in Kensington, to the circus, and, in deference to the sporting inclinations of both of us, to Highbury and Stamford Bridge and Harringay Arena and Wembley Stadium.

I have dim recollections of riding with him on trams in the early years, and I can certainly remember with perfect clarity a conversation we shared about their passing. We were returning home from Harringay late one night after the great Boon-Danahar fight for the British Lightweight title. It was the first-ever trolley-bus ride for both of us and we were disconcerted by the uncanny silence. Trams, on the other hand, rattled you to your destination. But the worst of their drawbacks was that it was hard to tell if they were drawing back or not. They were built to go either way, that is, they looked as if they had a front at each end and no behind anywhere at all. They used to go rumbling along Hampstead Road up towards the heights of Kentish Town, past two public houses which once stood on the eastern and western corners of the junction with Euston Road. When at eleven o'clock each night they poured the drunks out on to the pavements, the poor men would stagger about in the road staring at the trams passing by and not knowing which way anything was moving. They would attempt a leap in order to board a tram that hadn't reached them yet, and they would fling themselves into the gutter to avoid being hit by a tram that was actually receding from them. And if they did succeed in boarding, there were the seats to compound their confusion. These seats were reversible; by pushing the backrest you could contrive to make them face the other way round, which meant that if you happened to find yourself seated opposite a particularly repulsive specimen of Londoner, you could always push the back of your seat forward and sit facing an even more repulsive specimen of Londoner.

To all of us in those days, when a motor car was something so exotic that when one parked in a back street, half the neighbourhood would come out for a look, public transport was a dominant feature of life. A tram, or a bus, or a train, might mean the difference between salvation and damnation, or between consummation and frustration. There was the affecting case of a good friend of mine, Albert O, whose parents ran a small cafe in Euston Road. It was situated directly facing a bus-stop, and had one of those sliding-window affairs through which the proprietor could dispense ice cream and cold drinks to those customers too fastidious to venture inside. Albert O spent most of his adolescence manning that window. Often if I was playing truant and catching a No. 1 bus to the Dominion, Tottenham Court Road, or a No. 137 to the Gaumont, Camden Town, I would pass the time of day with him until my bus arrived. And he told me that years of empirical research had proved to his satisfaction that the girls who boarded the No. 134 had bigger breasts and better shapes than the girls who used the other services. He was unable to offer any explanation for this, but of the efficacy of the theory itself he had no doubt whatsoever. He subsequently confirmed his faith by marrying a well-endowed girl who lived up somewhere near Tufnell Park.

If the buses proved awkward, there was always the underground. Social historians have overlooked the immense advance in literacy represented by London's underground. In the days of buses and trams and even trolleys, the conductor would call out each location on arrival. But in the tube there was nothing to guide you but the carriage maps, which meant that passengers incapable of reading either had to learn how many stops it was to their destination and sit there counting – some of them couldn't count either – or ask perfect strangers where they were. There was also the question of claustrophobia. Yet another of my aunts, the hypochondriac, adamantly refused to travel on the underground at all, being convinced that the tunnels would collapse the moment the word got around that she was on board. Nothing anyone could say or do was enough to shake her conviction that once they got her underground they would keep her there. As an example of the hopelessness of her case, there is the story of the first-ever escalator to be installed on London's underground. This was at Earl's Court in 1911, and posed a tricky problem for the authorities. How could they convince the passenger that the whole thing wasn't part of a plot to rip off the soles of his shoes, transform his socks into balaclava helmets, and recycle him for use as an unguent? They could not very well close down the station, which was so often their tactic when faced with a problem. Nor could they remove the escalator, which had cost so much money to install. So they hit on a ploy of such brilliance as to rank among the great demonstrations of the English genius for pragmatism. They hired a man called Bumper Harris to go up and down the escalators all day, to encourage the others, as it were. Harris, you see, had only one leg, and it used to be said by my hypochondriac aunt that she had a bloody good idea what had happened to the other one.

Nobody ever really went to the roots of the myth of the underground. You used to hear stories of phantom stations and ghost lines which had probably originated in the jibbering of old ladies like my aunt. But sometimes rational, intelligent observers reported phenomena just as outlandish. One of the most thorough of all London newspaper reporters, H. V. Morton, once went down after midnight with the maintenance men:

> They wander on like explorers in an Egyptian tomb, and this resemblance is intensified by occasional mosquitoes which live in this even temperature all the year long. I did not see one. I am told, however, that gangers who go to sleep often awaken bitten; but as a stray ganger is the only brightness in the life of a tube mosquito, for they never penetrate to the richer potentialities of the stations, who shall grudge them an infrequent happiness.

I can just imagine my aunt saying I told you so to that, but Morton has more to come. One night he travels from Bow to Ealing, sitting next to the driver. Before reaching the end of the line, he finds himself in conversation with an inspector who has been working underground for thirty years:

> "Now of course, everything is bigger, quicker and better. You can have the good old days. I remember them and I prefer these. Why, bless my soul, in the good old days we had to have a regular baby hunt nearly every night under the seats of the old trains. Anybody who didn't want a baby seemed to leave it in the Underground."

But there was one trick that Morton and his inspector missed, and which I discovered much later, when, as a musician, I resided in a world constantly faced with the challenge of how to outface Mrs. Grundy. In the 1950s hypocritical hoteliers were still inclined to refuse admission to loving couples unless the ritual was first performed of a bogus name and address in the register and the waving of a sixpenny wedding ring. One day some unsung genius discovered a way round the problem. It appeared that of all conservative institutions in Britain, it was British Rail that was making the fornicating art a little easier. It was a fact of life so obvious that for years nobody noticed it, that the only respectable place in the country where a man could book a double room for the night and not be obliged to produce his partner and assume a fake identity was at the Sleeping Berth Reservation windows at King's Cross and St. Pancras. You simply booked the accommodation as far in advance as you wished, and eventually turned up with whoever you had tempted to travel with you. There was only one small drawback to the system, which was that you tended to wake up next morning in Glasgow. But a great many itinerant saxophonists and drummers of my acquaintance seemed happy enough to take their chances on the night trains to Scotland; indeed, the practice became so common that it has always amazed me that the following exchange never took place in an English divorce court:

> Judge: How many times did adultery take place?
> Defendant: Once, my lord.
> Judge: And where did it take place?
> Defendant: In Herts, Lincolnshire, Yorkshire, the Lake District and Angus, my lord.

In fact, it was the girls who were most liable to draw a young man, if not on to the night train at King's Cross, then at least to outlying parts of the town he might otherwise never have seen. I can recall "seeing home" girls to Ruislip and Charlton and Hackney and Hornsey and Wandsworth and Wembley. There was one girl I remember in particular, a secretary in one of the big recording companies, who, when I asked if I could take her home, replied cheerfully, "Yes, where do you live?" But that was just her repartee; the evening ended conventionally enough. She lived at Clapham Common, not a spot with which I was familiar. I had a vague idea that there was a large railway junction nearby which had once inspired a splendidly obscene limerick, but that connection with literature aside, my feelings as she bade me goodnight and trotted up a garden path not dissimilar to the one she had been leading me up all evening, were akin to those of the young man in the P. G. Wodehouse story who, when faced with the identical problem, said:

> The first thing to do is to ascertain that such a place as Clapham Common really exists. One has heard of it, of course, but has its existence ever been proved? I think not. Having accomplished that, we must then try to find out how to get to it. I should say at a venture that it would necessitate a sea voyage.

In the event it necessitated, not a sea voyage, but a long haul home on the all-night bus. Whether such conveyances survive I am not sure, but in my musical days, when the last waltz and the last bus tended to start at roughly the same time, the all-night service was a lifeline. There was a period in my life, after my amateur days were done but before I became a fully-fledged professional, when I played at innumerable dances and weddings in the suburban triangle described by Stoke Newington, Manor House and Clapton. A hundred times I picked up the all-nighter at the corner of Stamford Hill, to enter a tiny exclusive community whose existence I had never thought about before. On the upper deck were mostly charladies travelling in with lips cupid-bowed to clean out the offices of Whitehall. They generally hid their hair under kerchiefs and spoke with cigarettes dangling from their lips. Downstairs you found the occasional caretaker or burglar or printer, and of course the conductor, who always seemed to have adapted to his unsocial hours by becoming a sort of stand-up comic. Between 1949 and 1952, according to a careful record I kept, the conductors of all-night buses asked me the question, as they glanced at my instrument case, "Who've you got in there then?" forty eight times.

Later, when I became less of an all-purpose musician and more of a jazz specialist, working in the Soho jazz clubs, I would walk home in the small hours, often stopped by some policeman new to the beat, and occasionally meeting up with one of the rats who formed the Cleveland Street colony, and who would run about the pavements under the dim light of the Corporation lamps and vault over your shoes even as you skipped to avoid them. One of my associates during this fairly chaotic period of my life was the saxophonist Ronnie Scott, who was living on the top floor of a building just off Shaftesbury Avenue whose ground floor was famous as a long-established Indian restaurant. Sometimes after work we would retire to Scott's eyrie for coffee and gossip and hear scrabbling noises behind the skirting. The only person unperturbed by this eerie sound effect was Scott himself, who explained it away as the monthly rice war in which the rival groups of rat-residents of the building used to indulge. He would always manage to put a stop to the scrabbling by flinging a shoe at the wall. "One time," said Scott, with a perfectly straight face, "the Head Rat flung one back."

Being one of the oldest districts of London, Soho was in too dilapidated a condition to be renovated. Even the more famous night-clubs were really little more than grubby cellars tarted up by dim lighting and ambitious decor. The trouble was that often when you played in the band in one of these places, you were expected to eat there too, which exposed you to the same hideous diseases as the customers. It was always wise, therefore, to make a tour of the kitchens of your place of employment before ordering your supper. I once worked for two weeks and one day for an old-time bandleader called Lew Stone in one of the most famous night-clubs in London. The workman's entrance led through the kitchens to the bandroom, which meant that you could not help noticing the dreadful deeds being committed in the name of nourishment. It was always my firm conviction that I managed to sidestep serious illness only by sticking resolutely for thirteen nights on the trot to the following menu:

Monday	Spaghetti and cold water.
Tuesday	Spaghetti and cold water.
Wednesday	Spaghetti and cold water.
Thursday	Spaghetti and cold water.
Friday	Spaghetti and cold water.
Saturday	Spaghetti and cold water.

It was not very long after this that Scott opened his own club; when asked why, he said that after all these years of being swindled by promoters, he didn't see why he shouldn't swindle himself for a change. The premises were in a cellar in Gerrard Street, a thoroughfare not at that time noted for its connections with the Fine Arts. Once a week a few of us would hold a formal committee meeting, chaired by Scott, at which we decided on the text of the advertisements to be placed in the musical weekly comics. The reader should understand that a convention had developed among jazz promoters of inserting advertisements in the trade papers each week announcing their coming attractions, and that these advertisements had a look about them of having been composed by a convocation of small men standing in eight feet of water. I, for example, was quite often billed as "The World's Greatest Saxophonist," an untruth compared to which the claim that George Eliot was one of the Bronte Sisters fades into pallid actuality. There was not a working jazz musician who had not at some time been excruciatingly embarrassed by the adjectival falsehoods attached to his name in those papers. It might be Unbelievable, or Incredible, or Fabulous, or Phenomenal, but whatever it was, it was always a lie. Now that Scott was himself an entrepreneur he took his revenge. Any student who cares to look into the files of the musical press of the period will learn that the Scott Club ads are sociologically curious, and have about them the authentic ring of wild anarchy:

> Food untouched by human hand. Our chef is a gorilla.
> The best cuisine in town. Fifty million flies can't be wrong.
> This week: Ronnie Scott plays music from the film of the same name.

When times were hard Scott would advertise Menuhin with Strings, or Sonja Henie on Ice, or a lecture by the eminent Indian jazz expert Pandid Badly and his dapper friend Mahatma Coat. He even worked up the habit of announcing the imminent arrival on the bandstand of Toulouse-Lautrec, lowering the microphone to within a few inches of the ground and then leaving the stage. It is revealing that the only people who craned forward in expectation of a midget were the professional jazz critics. Everybody in the profession predicted an early collapse of Scott's. That was twenty two years ago and it is still rolling on.

Not all the inhabitants of that half-world of playing days were musicians; many of them were friends and hangers-on who enjoyed most of the fruits of the musical life without its drudgery. Usually they came and went, but there was one of these moral supporters, the great Jibber Gold, who deserves a footnote to the social history of modern London. The verb "to Jib", which, alas, has yet to rise to the respectability of a place in the dictionaries, means to gain entry to a place of public entertainment or private celebration without an invitation and without paying. Gold was the greatest master of this maligned art that there has ever been, and would set himself a target of five jibs a week just to keep himself up to the mark. There was a short period during 1958 when I ran a jazz club of my own at a venue called The Empire Rooms in Tottenham Court Road. And although Jibber, being an old friend of mine, was free to come and go as he wished, he used to make a point of jibbing in through the back entrance, strolling through the hall, out the front door and then round to the back again. When I asked him what his game was he told me somewhat loftily that although I might not be aware of the fact, there was such a thing as art for art's sake. Of course I might have put him on the official Free List along with the critics, journalists and the rest of the spongers, but that would have spoiled his fun and inhibited the practice of his art. I well remember a girl in our crowd planning the guest-list for her twenty-first and saying, "Oh, we must have Jibber. Make a note not to send him an invitation."

Jibber's finest hour came with the opening in 1951 of the Royal Festival Hall. Being a brand new venue, with unknown procedures and unfamiliar routines, it seemed in Jibber's eyes to possess the sort of attraction that A. J. Raffles must have found in a row of pearls. He went about his work like the artist he was, getting to know the workings of the service lifts, the habits of the doormen, the location of the fire escapes. Then, having cased the joint to his own satisfaction, he prevailed upon his father, an innocent back-street tailor of the old school, to make him an exact facsimile of a Royal Festival Hall commissionaire's uniform, including the peaked cap and the campaign ribbons. It turned out to be the very pinnacle not only of Jibber's art but of his father's too, for the other commissionaires, misled by an excess of gold braid in which the old man had indulged, not only allowed the son to pass unmolested but were inclined to salute him. This unseen development stung Jibber to the roots of his democratic soul, and not very long afterwards the end came when he accidentally discovered that, because of some obscure by-law down among the small print at County Hall, the commissionaires at the Royal Festival Hall were disbarred from actually physically handling an interloper. After that the fun went out of it for him, and he retired from jibbing. Some years later he attempted a comeback with his supreme masterpiece, the Reverse Jib, whereby you paid for admission to some event and then jibbed OUT even though the ushers had been instructed to see that nobody left his seat during the performance.

It is difficult to unravel truth from fancy when it comes to a witness like Jibber, but he told me years later how he had happened to stumble on this new masterplan. One evening, finding himself at a loose end, he wandered over to the Royal Festival Hall to find a Dave Brubeck concert in progress. Now Jibber, for all his non-musical preoccupations, was always a good judge of music, and in the normal way would never have been seen dead at such an event. But it had been a long time since he had last attempted a jib, and even as he gazed through the glass windows into the foyer, the soul of a born jibber urged him to make his entry. Which he did, in mid-performance. Twenty minutes later, with the same piano solo still proceeding, Jibber, by now half-crazed from the repetition, decided to go home, only to find his way blocked by an army of officious ushers. "Think how awful it would of been," he said to me, "if I'd of paid to get in." He went home that night and brooded on his experience long and hard, finally coming up with the plan which he believed would make him rich beyond the dreams of average, as the saying goes. What he would do would be to open a club, admission free. Then he would book someone like Brubeck and charge the customers a fiver to get OUT. Nothing came of the idea, but I often think of it, and him, whenever I see a juke box with facilities for buying three minutes of silence.

Throughout these years the ripples had been spreading ever wider across the face of the urban lake. In my teens I had trudged the streets of St. Marylebone and St. Pancras, there and back, there and back, debating some cosmic frivolity or other with fiercely committed friends. As a musician I had plied for hire at places as removed in geography and as disparate in spirit as the Tufnell Park Palais and the Galtymore Irish Dance Club in Cricklewood; the Royal, Tottenham and the Hammersmith Palais; Churchill's in Bond Street and the Locarno in Streatham High Street. Every Saturday night for one whole winter I played in a band at the Municipal Hall, Tottenham, where the lucky girl who won the raffle on Ladies' Night was allowed to kiss the musician of her choice. Every week it was the same. The winning ticket number would be announced, its owner would announce herself with a squeal of excitement, she would come and take a look at the band, and then start crying. I had attended evening classes as a student in Holborn and as a lecturer in

Balham and at New Cross. I had made the discovery that London stretched from Wimbledon to Stanmore, and from Twickenham to Greenwich, and that a curious thing was happening to it; as the edges expanded, so the centre was emptying. There was constant peripheral gain, paid for by a canker at the heart. I began to be sentimental about back streets which all my life I had taken for granted. One day the bulldozers came and knocked down my childhood. The little window at which Albert O had made his discoveries in Comparative Anatomy, the old Oil shop, my old school, my old flats, my old everything, down they went, until, at a preternaturally early age I found myself rootless, a man unable to point to a building and claim that that was where I had done a certain thing, or had a certain thing done to me. All my life I had heard old men making the same complaint, that once They whoever They happened to be, destroyed your environment, what was left to prove you had ever passed that way at all? The Blitz had started it, the planners finished it, until at last you were surprised to find yourself defending some obscure corner of the town which, ordinary as it was, had suddenly assumed towering, symbolic significance.

Mention of the Blitz recalls for me memories of my hypochondriac aunt, the OTHER hypochondriac aunt, that is. During the war, when the air raids were at their worst and the rest of the population of the town was scurrying nightly for the shelters, she stayed put in her second-floor flat near Regent's Park. Of course she should not have stayed there. She might have been blown to pieces. Or buried under rubble. Or frazzled by fire-bombs. But though she knew all this, still she refused to join the panicking hordes. This was not, however, a measure of her heroism or even of her foolhardiness. The fact was that she braved the perils of the bombs because out there in the streets was something that REALLY scared the pants off her. The block of flats where she lived – if you could call it living – was no more than a mile from the Regent's Park Zoo, and my aunt, having been surrounded by gambling brothers for as long as she could remember, which was usually about ten minutes, figured that it was no more than seven-to-four-against that one of these nights a bomb would drop on the Zoological Gardens and release all the inmates, who would instantly celebrate their sudden freedom by making a beeline for her. Why they should wish to do this neither my aunt nor any living zoologist was able to say, but she remained convinced of it throughout the war, dismissing newspaper reports of the removal of the more dangerous animals to distant parts as enemy propaganda. She firmly believed, she told me, that on some nights, after a fierce raid, the black mambas had got out and were even now slinking silently up the cracked stone steps of the flats, looking forward to their buffet supper of raw aunt. And it was a waste of time double-locking her front door because the elephants would only trample it down. She reckoned that one night she had actually seen a brown bear loafing in the shadows of a doorway in Cleveland Street. (This was true enough, but it turned out to be Old Man Marks, who had accidentally locked himself out after dumping some obsolescent pickled herrings in the dustbin.) She also said that she often heard the screech owls directing the eagles towards her, and during the buzz-bomb threat of 1944 began to get especially morbid fears about the gibbons and orang-utangs, whom she expected nightly, watching for them as they rode in triumph along Marylebone Road transported in troop-carriers, that is, in the pockets of the marsupials. The jackals, of course, would come last of all, but my aunt wasn't much worried about them, because by the time they deemed it prudent to put in an appearance, she reckoned she would already have gone to the Great Doctor's Waiting Room in the sky. One time, my uncle decided that if he sent her down to Bournemouth for a week, both of them might be able to get some sleep. But that didn't work out either; she was back the next morning, much chastened by the experience of sighting the Loch Ness Monster bearing down on Poole Harbour. It was odd that in all her terrors she never once mentioned lions and tigers, which are the creatures usually singled out by screwballs. But she had read somewhere that lions and tigers only kill when they are hungry, and for that contingency kept a few tins of Snoek at the ready. (For the benefit of the younger generation, Snoek was a wartime concoction of tinned whalemeat which certain members of the government kept insisting tasted just like food. The population remained unconvinced, including my aunt, who celebrated VE Day in the unshakeable conviction that all through the fighting Vera Lynn had been under orders from the Home Office to plug Snoek by singing incessantly "Whalemeat again, don't know where, don't know when..")

As the planners completed the work of despoliation begun by the Luftwaffe, I began to develop a sentimental interest in the history of the town, and realised more than ever before that whatever else you said about London, you had to admit that no city in history had been more fortunate in its chroniclers. Sometimes the chroniclers themselves had been less fortunate. The greatest of them, Charles Dickens, was a victim most of his life to an intensity of insomnia that not even my aunts could have imagined. And the Dickensian cure for sleeplessness was to walk the streets and squares of London with such energy and with such restlessness that at last the victim became one of the few men, I believe, who came close to grasping the complete, comprehensive essence of London. His idea of a good time was "a good brisk walk over Hampstead Heath, seven or eight miles"; during the composition of "A Christmas Carol" he was found "walking about the black streets of London fifteen and twenty miles many a night when all the sober folks have gone to bed." One night in 1857, after a family argument had made home intolerable, he rose from bed at two o'clock in the morning, dressed, and "tramped all the thirty miles to Gad's Hill through the dead of night." London was at once his source-book and his plot-reservoir. He had only to stride a few blocks to find his theme for the next day's work; perhaps the sight of a derelict house, or a pool of lamplight shining down on a waif; a shop-front, a mangy cat, a barrow of fruit, a wall spattered with flapping posters, the echo of a fiddle wafting through the stage-door of some suburban playhouse, anything was enough to set his senses racing. Somebody once said that Dickens knew the town better than any man "from Bow to Brentford," and the student of such affairs will find much of that recondite knowledge in "Sketches by Boz," in which we read of "the bulldog in a shy corner of Hammersmith who keeps a man," a pair of speckled hens in Bethnal Green to whom, "gaslight was quite as natural as any other light," and who were so quick to pick up the habits of the locals that "they always begin to crow when the public-house shutters begin to be taken down." He reports children frisking in Burlington Arcade, mentions "the awful perspectives of Harley and Wimpole Streets," and passes an old City warehouse "which rotting paste and rotting paper had brought down to the condition of an old cheese."

One of his favourite haunts was the River, not just the dank, fetid mausoleum of "Our Mutual Friend," but also the sparkling, convivial river down at Greenwich. Dickens was by no means the only Victorian to associate Greenwich with champagne and the good-time life. Members of the cabinet used to celebrate the ending of a parliamentary session by partaking of a whitebait supper down there. (Whitebait was especially plentiful at Greenwich in those days, and the reason, which was said to be to do with the amount of filth and garbage in the water, also suggests why so many politicians found it congenial.) Dickens loved the area so passionately that while he was in America delivering his lectures, he would sometimes pause in mid-mouthful in some rowdy hotel salon and, while Yankees on all sides expectorated with deadly accuracy into numberless spittoons, dream of whitebait at Greenwich. On his return from his first American tour, his friends organised a welcome-home supper for him at his favourite Greenwich inn; among the guests was the artist Cruikshank, who drank so much that Dickens was obliged to pour him into his own cab and drive him home as gently as possible. Cruikshank made this difficult by insisting on standing on his head all the way back to Marylebone, and suffered such a searing hangover the following morning that he took an oath of teetotalism and never drank again for the rest of his life.

Other writers regarded Greenwich in a slightly less flattering light. As a young critic Bernard Shaw went there one night in 1889 with his friend and fellow-critic William Archer. They were to see a long-running musical called "Dorothy," only to learn on arrival that the performance was sold out, except for standing room in the pit. This posed a problem, because Archer had been a critic for so long that by now he only went to theatres in order to get a good sleep. To sleep standing up in the pit posed no serious problem for him, but it did pose one for everyone else. Archer always had violent nightmares

when sleeping standing up, and there was a very real danger that he might disrupt the show even more disastrously than the cast had been doing for the past 788 performances. At last the management found the two critics a pair of seats high in the gallery. Once the show began, Shaw hated it even more than he expected to, saying of the leading man that he was "evidently counting the days until death should release him from his contract." The high spot of the show was supposed to be the moment when a pack of real live dogs run on to the stage:

> The pack of hounds darted in at the end of the second act evidently full of the mad hope of finding something new going on. And their depression when they discovered it was "Dorothy" again was pitiable. The RSPCA should interfere. If there is no law to protect men and women from "Dorothy," there is at least one that can be strained to protect dogs.

Long before the curtain, the two young men had stolen away, passing the time on the journey back to the West End by wondering what life must be like for a performer trapped in a show like "Dorothy." Shaw decided that the cast couldn't possibly die on stage. "The actors first become mad and are removed to an asylum, where they sing their parts incessantly till death seals their tortured ears forever." Shaw's talk of insanity evokes thoughts of the great humorist Beachcomber, who tells the story of a young country bumpkin who applied for a job at Greenwich Observatory and was accepted. On his first morning he was taken into the presence of a world-famous astronomer, and watched the old boy training a huge telescope on the heavens. At that moment a shooting star perforated the sky, at which the apprentice clapped his hands and shouted, "That was a good shot, sir."

But the river at Greenwich is only one Thames among dozens. In fact the Thames has as many personalities as there have been writers attracted to it. Outstanding among these was W. W. Jacobs, in whose stories gnarled old maritime reprobates suck on foul pipes in dozing waterside pubs and dispense philosophy to the effect that the world might be a more comfortable place if only the fates could work out a way of running it without women, and that considering the unfortunate nature of prevailing circumstances, it is a wonder that sailors manage to remain as pure and as honourable as they do – "Sailormen 'ave their faults," said the nightwatchman frankly. "I'm not denying of it. I used to 'ave 'em myself when I was at sea." But Jacobs himself was not really interested in the sea, only in what happened when men came home from it. His fictions move between the grubby lodginghouses of the Port of London and the little lazy towns along the Thames estuary, and their creator observes with a shrewd if cynical eye the antics of sailors caught in the limbo between one long voyage and the next. If ever a man needed the tumult and gusto of a town to feed his imagination, then that man was Jacobs and that town London. When, as a married man he moved his family to Berkhamsted, he dried up into a terrible object-lesson for every Londoner who feels he may be ready to shuffle off the influence of his home town. You can never shuffle London off, as Jacobs discovered. He grew to hate Hertfordshire – "too many cows" – and besides, the county had no sailors in its public houses. Jacobs never rediscovered the flavour of the life he had been born to in Wapping, but the stories, bitterly comic, have survived, preserving a picture of a way of life that has vanished.

The obverse of the medal may be found in the work of Jacobs' contemporary and fellow East Ender H.M. Tomlinson, whose Thames is without broad humour but lit with sly wit. Born in Poplar, and employed in boyhood as a clerk in a shipping office, Tomlinson escaped into journalism, completed certain famous voyages in modest working ships, and wrote some of the most exquisite tributes to the life of a great seagoing city that have ever been published. Tomlinson lived through one of the saddest revolutions in the history of the Port of London, the transition from sail to steam. He saw that steam was inevitable, but mourned the death of what he took to be genuine seamanship as distinct from the manipulation of dials and pistons. As a lad he had sometimes been entrusted with documents relevant to the departure of some cargo boat, and never forgot, throughout a long life, the sensation of walking along the wharves "under an arcade of bowsprits" and feeling reassured that the world generally and London in particular must be a rich and generous place indeed, because as he trudged along seeking out this or that merchantman, he found that the very paving stones along which he marched were strewn with sugar and molasses and spices, the priceless detritus of a mercantile city. Tomlinson loved Dockland with the kind of passion that finds poetry in apparently mundane things. Tomlinson found it in the names of the streets of Dockland, names which fired his insular imagination and fuelled his dreams of one day sailing in the same ships whose names he inscribed in his ledgers. Which were the more evocative, the local street names, Malabar, Amoy, Nankin, Canton, Pekin, or the ships themselves, Rajah of Cochin, Lincelles, Euterpe, Wangunai, Waimea, Hermione? Even the grim-looking inlets along the Port of London sounded chords in Tomlinson's head, and more than once he intoned them, Bugsby's, Blackwall, Gallion's, like a litany.

His river was the working Thames, the tidal river, and you would no more think of it in terms of the larky bubbling farcical Thames of Jerome K. Jerome's Three Men in a Boat than you would picture W. W. Jacobs flying the Atlantic. In terms of mere mileage, compared to, say, the Amazon or the Mississippi, the Thames may seem like a backwater, but because its complexion changes so rapidly and so completely, sometimes within a few hundred yards, it has won the reputation of being one of the world's most intriguing waterways. Jerome's Three Men, the silly-ass late-Victorian bachelors, established the fame of Hampton Court so utterly

that from the day the book was published, people thought of the place as the location of the Maze where the foolish are lost, and no longer in terms of the burglarious tendencies of Henry VIII. Most of Jerome's book drifts lazily out of London's orbit, away into the river at Marlow and at last up to Oxford. But it is impossible to say at which point precisely either the river or Jerome's book ceases to belong to London. Less contentious is the river of A.P. Herbert, the river on whose playful surface bob houseboats so landlocked that six days a week the local postman delivers the letters. Herbert is the only considerable modern writer to have actually lived on the river, in a houseboat conveniently close to Westminster, where he sat for years as an Independent Member when he should have been doing more• important work at his typewriter. In "The Water Gipsies," Herbert wrote one of the better London novels, about the kind of townees who are often dismissed by noodles as "ordinary folk," the kind who go to the dogs on Saturday night, eat fish and chips or jellied eels on the way home, take trips on barges, love beer and bank holidays, and, without giving it a thought, typify the town that bred them.

One of the main characters in "The Water Gipsies" is a painter, but the reader gets the distinct impression that he is not a very good one. Whether his work was better than that of the real painters who have inhabited the waterfront at various times is doubtful. The greatest of them was the American wisecracking expatriate Jimmy Whistler, who combined with Oscar Wilde to make Tite Street, Chelsea, famous, and who compared the river there to Venice. Around the corner was Whistler's friendly enemy Dante Gabriel Rossetti, who occupied a house in Cheyne Walk in the days before the Embankment was built. That meant that there was a real foreshore at the water's edge, and Rossetti could always tell when it was high tide because the water would rise up and flood his cellar. Being an idealist, Rossetti had the quaint idea of gathering a menagerie at Cheyne Walk, and with this end in view, took a lenient attitude towards the rats in the cellar, whom he used to feed on kippers. One day his pet wombat ate the straw hat of one of his lady models, and the large white bull he installed in the back garden quickly destroyed the lawn. His peacocks took a dim view of this, and the kangaroos and armadillos became so upset that Rossetti had to build wooden huts for them to sleep in. As for the squirrels, owls, mice and dormice, they spent much time inside the house, and Rossetti would feed them on raw eggs.

His dream of an Eden in Chelsea soon foundered, when the youngest of the kangaroos succumbed to a fit of Oedipal rage and bumped off its own mother. The racoon then killed the killer, after which it began to wander afield and feed on the eggs laid by neighbours' chickens. One of the armadillos, finding itself depressed by the diet of raw eggs, dug its way under the house and burrowed up through the floor of the kitchen of the house next door, causing the cook of the establishment to pack her bags immediately and take an oath of teetotalism. Finally, a crisis was reached when one of the fallow deer, bored with having nothing to do, began chasing the last surviving peacock, trampled on its feathers and caused the poor bird to shriek and scream all day. The local inhabitants began complaining, which is understandable enough in the light of the hideous eldritch cries of which the peacock is capable, all of which explains why to this very day, even though Dante Gabriel and his four-legged friends have long since vanished, the Cadogen Estate inserts a clause in all its leases of the houses in Cheyne Walk barring residents from keeping pet peacocks.

That entanglement of past habits and present laws is typical of a town which has been civilised for so long that nobody can remember any more how half its by-laws ever came about. To this day the casual pedestrian may easily break the law without realising it, for instance by wheeling a perambulator down Burlington Arcade, or even whistling in that august promenade. (I once tried the experiment of wheeling a perambulator down it AND whistling at the same time, but nothing happened, either to me or the perambulator.) The past also impinges, though in a very different way, on the status of that sad stone, Cleopatra's Needle, which has been pointing up to the heavens at Charing Cross for more than a century now. The stone, which has about as much to do with Cleopatra as I do, was erected on its present site in 1878, and thereby hangs a tale. When the London authorities erected it, they placed under its foundations a collection of sealed jars whose function was to be what a later age usually describes as a Time capsule. In these jars were placed for the edification of posterity, a man's lounge suit, the complete dress and vanities of a lady of fashion, illustrated papers, bibles, toys, cigars, a set of coins of the realm, and photographs of the most beautiful women of the day. A century later I modestly suggested that it might be enlightening to dig up the sealed jars, but nobody took any notice, leaving me to wonder who they chose at the time to select the most beautiful women in England, and what his qualifications were.

The past obtrudes in a different way on my old stamping grounds in Euston. There is, as travellers will know, an underground station called Euston Square but no thorough-fare of that name. The explanation comes from that inveterate literary gossip Ford Madox Ford, who as a child took violin lessons from a man called Borschitzky who lived in Euston Square. The old boy came home one night to find his landlady murdered in the kitchen, and, being almost blind, tripped over the corpse and got himself covered in her blood. Being a musician, he was, of course, instantly arrested and accused of the murder, but was subsequently acquitted. But the trial caused such a frisson of horror to pulsate through London that residents of the Square petitioned to have its name changed, which it was, and remains to this day, as Endsleigh Gardens. Whether Ford is an altogether reliable witness is another question. He often allowed the

storyteller's art to run away with the truth, as appears to have happened in the following anecdote:

I had a very elderly and esteemed relative who once told me that while walking along the Strand he met a lion that had escaped from the menagerie at the old Exeter Exchange. I said, "What did you do?" and he looked at me with contempt, as if the question were imbecile. "Do?" he said, "Why, I took a cab."

Ford's story about Endsleigh Gardens, true or false, raises the issue of who christens London's streets and why. The main factor seems to be Fame, although not always in the expected order of precedence. For example, while Benjamin Disraeli currently rates only four roads and a close, his arch rival Gladstone gets eight roads, four avenues, a mount, a street and a park gardens. Both of them, however, are outclassed by Lord Palmerston who, apart from public houses without number, can boast fifteen roads, two crescents and a grove. Among the other front runners in the London Streetname Stakes, the following will give some idea of the inclinations of London's rulers:

Queen Victoria 91; the Duke of Wellington 48; Lord Nelson 37; Cromwell 32; Shakespeare 20; Churchill 14; Field Marshal Montgomery 7; Charles Dickens 6.

Even more revealing than the names of London's streets are the decorations that festoon them. The game of the Blue Plaques, in which the investigator searches out the homes of people so honoured, is even more revealing than the Street Name ploy. It was the plaques which instructed me when I was a small boy, that I lived in a district honoured many times by the presence of people who later became distinguished. Frankly, this bewildered me. Why would a distinguished person wish to live in our district? Why for example, should Samuel Morse, inventor of the code that bears his name, pitch camp in Cleveland Street? Why William Pitt in Baker Street and why James Boswell in Great Portland Street? I could understand H.G. Wells in Hanover Terrace, because Hanover Terrace, overlooking the ducks of Regent's Park, was what the estate agents used to describe in their blowsy prose as a salubrious location. The plaque most familiar of all was the one in Fitzroy Square commemorating the fact that in the days of his young manhood, when he was living on apples, cocoa and cold porridge, Shaw conducted his one-man revolution from a second-floor bolthole just round the corner from where I lived. Like Ford Madox Ford, Shaw sometimes gilded the lily a bit in reminiscing about his days in the Square, but like Ford again, he gilded with such artistry that it is doubtful if posterity cares. One night in his theatre reviewing days, Shaw went to the Alhambra to see a famous dancer called Vincenti, who specialised in performing a series of spinning pirouettes. On returning home, still half-drunk on Vincenti's virtuosity, Shaw sees that it is past midnight, and that the Square, bathed in moonlight, is deserted. He decides to try to pirouette for himself, because "the circular railing round the Square presented such a magnificent hippodrome." Shaw soon finds that the trick is more difficult than it looks:

> After my fourteenth fall I was picked up by a policeman. "What are you doing here?" he said, keeping fast hold of me. "I bin watching you for the last five minutes." I explained, eloquently and enthusiastically. He hesitated a moment and then said, "Would you mind holding my helmet while I have a try. It don't look so hard."

The policeman then makes his attempt and has soon torn his trousers on the macadam. But like Shaw he is stiffened by resolve and keeps at it. At four o'clock in the morning an Inspector arrives and asks the policeman if this is his idea of fixed point duty, to which the policeman replies, "I allow it ain't fixed point, but I'll lay half a sovereign YOU can't do it." Naturally the Inspector soon joins in and after half an hour or so had begun to make progress. At which point Shaw tacitly admits that the whole thing is an invention by deliberately lapsing from the implausible to the downright slapstick:

> We were subsequently joined by an early postman and by a milkman, who unfortunately broke his leg and had to be carried to hospital by the other three. By that time I was quite exhausted, and could barely crawl into bed.

An even more interesting train of thought is opened up by a pair of plaques in Park Street, Mayfair, where the unsuspecting researcher is flabbergasted to find the only memorial in London ever put up for lying down, the honoured party being Catherine "Skittles" Walters, whose inscription reads, with admirable candour, "The Last of the Courtesans." Skittles, who occupied a great many coroneted beds during the later Victorian era, shares her posthumous residence in Park Street with another eminent Victorian lady, who lived across the road, Florence Nightingale, leaving posterity to savour the piquancy of the juxtaposition and to ponder the vexed question of which of these two formidable ladies gave mankind the greater bodily relief. A pairing just as ribald but of a very different style may be found in Horseguards Parade, where the twin statues of Field Marshals Roberts and Wolseley are located fifty paces apart. Each of these Victorian heroes stares pointedly due west, thereby avoiding the other's eye, a situation which hints at the fact that much as Roberts and Wolseley hated the infidel, that hatred was nothing compared to the detestation they felt for each other. Each one heartily wished the other dead many times, and it must be accounted one of London's richest jokes that in death the two sworn enemies should end up so uncomfortably close.

But neither Shaw, nor Skittles, nor Roberts nor Wolseley, nor any of the other real-life residents of London can compare for sheer fame and romance to the man I have not mentioned so far, the most widely-known person ever to set foot in the town and yet who never existed. All over the world disputatious scholars battle out rival theories as to the true location of Number 221B Baker Street, the one-time residence of Mr. Sherlock Holmes, the world's first consulting detective. Men have drawn maps, studied excavations, consulted gazetteers, read histories, all in an attempt to prove that Holmes's residence was at such-and-such a house. Some of their theories are so brilliantly intelligent that the unbiased reader is forced to the conclusion that the whole bunch of them are off their heads. The only man who might have answered the question, Sir Arthur Conan Doyle, died without disclosing the secret in 1933, since which time the world at large and American devotees in particular, have continued to adopt Holmesian methods of deduction to trace the house where Holmes himself practised. The Holmes stories are crammed with allusion after allusion to London streets or sometimes whole networks of streets, and the present writer is particularly thankful for the story entitled "The Blue Carbunkle," whose action begins with the stealing of a goose in Goodge Street, a thoroughfare so well-known to him that twice in his teens he fell in love for the last time within its limits. As to the correct location of Holmes's house, the issue remains of such importance to the followers all over the world who still write to him in an attempt to solicit his help, that it would be unthinkable for London to turn its back. In fact, the location of 221B was long ago agreed by the rational to have been on the site of the present Abbey National building in Baker Street. All letters addressed to Holmes are sent there, and the company has been enlightened enough to employ a man whose sole duty it is to answer these letters in the same reverently Holmesian spirit in which they were written.

The fascinations and whimsicalities of London are endless. So are its grandeurs and its shames, its genius and its foolishness, its beauty and its ugliness. (One day someone will compile a guide-book listing its most obnoxious aspects, and surely include the new Elephant and Castle, New Oxford Street and Kingsway, a thoroughfare so pointless that it is no longer possible to cross it, let alone live in it.) London remains an impenetrable mystery. Mark Twain once observed that "I had just as soon die in poverty in London as anywhere." His countryman Henry James came to the conclusion that "London is the heart of the world, and I prefer to be the least bit in its whirl than to live in and own a territory in any other place." A third American writer, Conrad Aiken, went further by saying "There is a dark, wonderful mystery of unknown London, the city of cities." But then again, tourists are always inclined to be a little too gushing for the taste of the undemonstrative Londoner, so perhaps it is more appropriate to close this reflection on the town that so obligingly raised me by quoting yet again its greatest reporter. In the summer of 1846, Dickens and his family were staying near Genoa. The novelist was in the throes of completing "Dombey and Son" and was finding the going hard. "Dombey and Son" happens to be a book permeated even more than is usual in Dickens by the spirit of the streets and squares within strolling distance of his home at that time, in Devonshire Terrace, on the corner of Marylebone Road. And in writing to his close friend and literary confidant, John Forster, Dickens said a very revealing thing about the extent of his difficulties in completing the book and the degree to which they were linked to his absence from the city of cities:

> The difficulty of going on at what I call a rapid pace is prodigious; it is almost an impossibility. I suppose this is partly the effect of two years' ease, and partly of the absence of streets and numbers of figures. I can't express how much I want these. It seems as if they supplied something to my brain, which it cannot bear, when busy, to lose. For a week or a fortnight I can write prodigiously in a retired place, and a day in London sets me up and starts me. But the toil and labour of writing, day after day, without that magic lantern, is immense.

Dickens clearly felt, as all sons of London feel, that when a man is away from London, then history is passing him by. History certainly moved from one epoch to the next in my own life one time, in a tableau which has always seemed to me typically London, in the impertinence, the shrewdness, the sly celebration of the ridiculous, which characterises it. One morning in the early 1950s I went for a haircut to an old youth club associate who had metamorphosed into a local institution called Syd the Barber. His emporium was a flyblown, dusty parlour behind Euston Station, its age incalculable, its three huge chairs of a minatory aspect which drew jokes about Sweeney Todd on an average four times a day, its soul buried beneath the hirsute droppings of generations of the shaved and barbered. I sat in one of the three chairs and for a while was pleased to contemplate my reflected self in a mirror bordered by cards and bits of paper advertising this or that pomade or hair restorer. (It was hard to believe in the efficacy of either, because Syd himself smelt like Old Man Marks' cucumber barrel and had gone bald at the age of sixteen from the sheer shock of going to work.) The moments passed. There was silence except for the clatter of the clippers on the nape of my neck, the snicker-snacker of the shears on my forelock, and, behind the clouded glass of the shopfront, the hum of desultory backstreet traffic. At last Syd the Barber broke the silence with a long sigh followed by a challenge, for the price of a haircut, to name the reigning monarch. I gave us both a long hard look in the mirror. What villainy was this? Even-money to name the King? Child's play. Taking a deep breath, I said, with some deliberation. "George the Sixth, that's a dollar you owe me." Without so much as a flicker of animation, he continued snipping away as he said, "Wrong. They announced his death on the wireless three minutes before you walked in here. Long live the Queen and that's a dollar you owe me." I told him to put it on the slate, and that is where it stayed for the next twenty five years, until at last the little shop followed the late King and Albert O's ice-cream window and the cucumber barrel and the black mambas and Goochie's bowler and the Oil shop and the assorted phobias of my assorted aunts into the vast stockpot of London lore, where they will remain until such time as there is nobody left alive to remember them, when they will be replaced by other recollections of other waves of Londoners, time without end, for ever and ever amen.

Benny Green

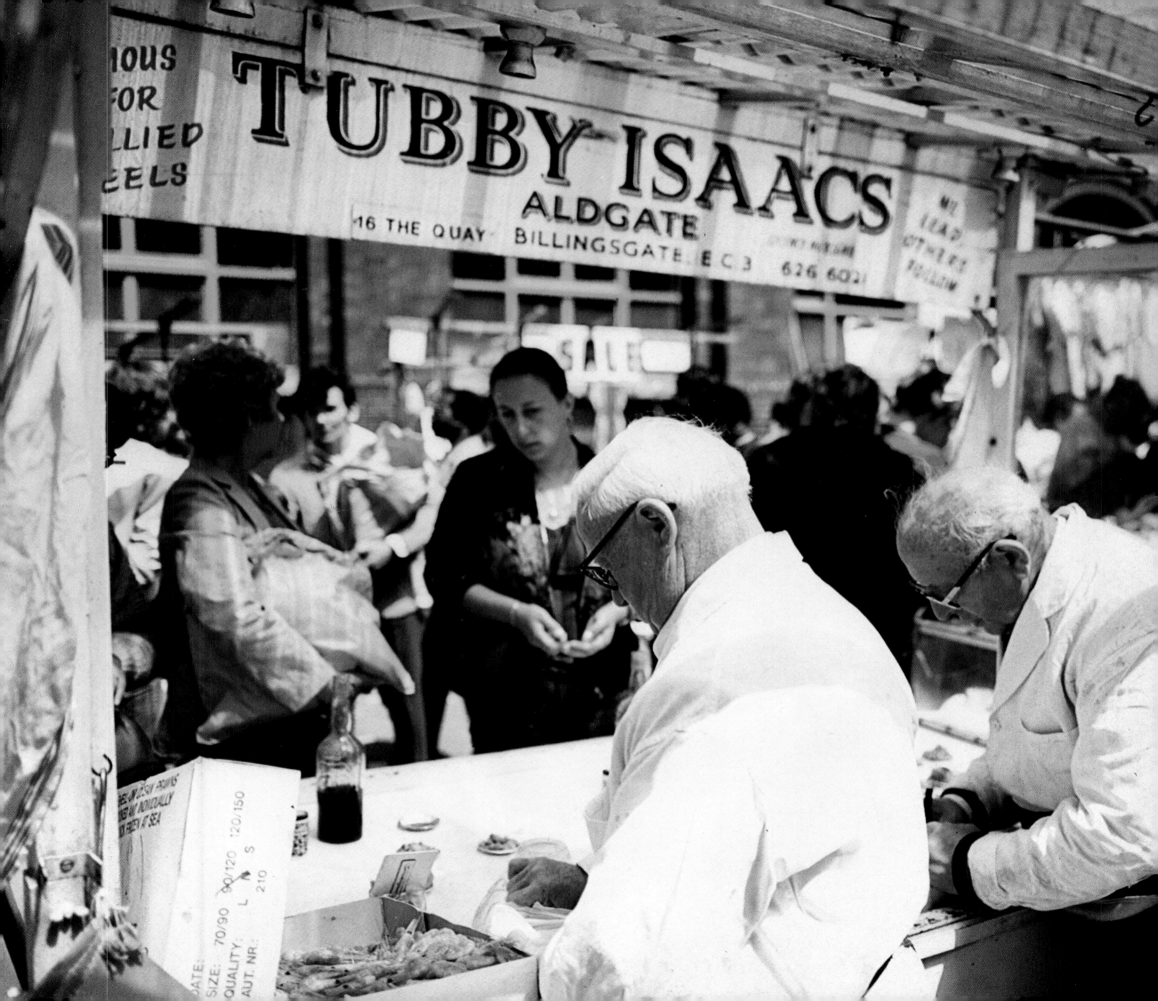

Eleven road bridges span the River Thames between Battersea and the Tower of London. Tower Bridge is undoubtedly the most well-known, and often confused with London Bridge, which was rebuilt in 1972 and, compared with Tower Bridge, is a rather ordinary structure.

The most modern of those pictured here (though not by many years) is Waterloo Bridge *left* which commands the best view of the heart of London. Albert Bridge and Chelsea Bridge *above* are, by contrast, delicate, and imaginatively lit by night. Lambeth Bridge *right*, completed in 1932, is adorned with pineapples as a tribute to John Tradescant, gardener to Charles I, who introduced the fruit into this country. He is buried nearby in St Mary's, Parish Church of Lambeth.

A symbol of peace stands in the middle of an area which can be described as anything but peaceful – Hyde Park Corner! The Wellington Arch, surmounted by a bronze chariot driven by a figure representing Peace *above*, was raised in celebration of the victory of the Duke of Wellington at Waterloo. The Arch itself contains a police station and is situated on an island around which travel over one hundred vehicles per minute.

The roads are rarely quiet in central London. *Right* Parking, even during the early evening, is always a problem. In Trafalgar Square *far right* empty taxis and buses wait to collect their night-time fares.

The sea of umbrellas *facing page* is a common
sight at London's major sporting events, but
rain never deters the spectators who are often
as anxious to catch sight of any members of
the Royal Family who might attend as they are
to watch the events themselves.

The skies open and the covers are pulled over the courts at Wimbledon *above*, the world's most prestigious tennis tournament, while *right* is sport of a different kind, as guests jostle and queue to meet the Queen and the Duke of Edinburgh at one of their summer garden parties. With a guest list of 9,000 at each party, it is unlikely that more than a handful will have the privilege of talking with them. The beautiful grounds of Buckingham Palace, a huge oasis in the heart of London, contain one of the largest lawns in the world.

The Royal Family are very fond of horse racing, the three major events of the year being Gold Cup Day at Ascot, and the Derby and Oaks races at Epsom. *Facing page* Home of the Surrey Cricket Club, the Oval at Kennington, near Vauxhall Bridge, is also the venue for international (test) matches and the last one of the season is generally played here.

The Ascot and Epsom race meetings are events people attend to 'see and be seen' as well as to watch the sport, and the ladies rise to the occasion with sometimes outrageous but always stunning outfits and hats. It is customary to take a picnic lunch and these are the times when a cheese sandwich and can of beer or lemonade simply won't do!

London's two premier churches differ greatly in style, but are equally beautiful. St Paul's Cathedral *above* was built by Sir Christopher Wren to replace the mediaeval church of Old St Paul's which was lost in the Great Fire of London in 1666. Completed in 1710, the Cathedral is of Portland stone, Renaissance in style, with twin baroque towers. The unmistakable dome is the second largest in the world, the largest being that of St Peter's in Rome. There have been five churches on this historic site, three of which were destroyed by fire – a fate which almost befell the present St Paul's during the bombing of London in World War II.

Westminster Abbey *above* has been the setting for the coronation of most English sovereigns since William the Conqueror, who was crowned here on Christmas Day in 1066. The Abbey is a 'royal peculiar,' meaning that it comes under the jurisdiction of a Dean and Chapter who are appointed by the monarch rather than by the Archbishop of Canterbury or the Bishop of London. The interior of the Abbey is magnificent; its chapels and aisles are filled with monuments and memorials and contain the tombs of most of Britain's rulers up to the 18th century. The roof of the Choir *right* is, like the rest of the Abbey, decorated with elaborate traceries and bosses.

St Paul's Cathedral was, in 1981, the scene of what has been called the "Wedding of the Century" – that of HRH The Prince of Wales to The Lady Diana Spencer. The choice of St Paul's represented a break with tradition, as most royal weddings have taken place in Westminster Abbey. Nevertheless, St Paul's was a popular choice, its size and spaciousness highlighting the exquisite mosaics and paintings throughout the interior. Another advantage was that St Paul's is rather larger than the Abbey – an important consideration when trying to pare down the guest list! These photographs show the splendid interior of this 'parish church of the British Commonwealth'.

The High Altar *left* and *right* was erected in 1958 to replace a reredos (altar screen) so damaged by bombing in World War II that it was beyond repair. The High Altar is of marble with a carved oak baldacchino. Behind it we see the magnificent mosaic of Christ in Majesty.

Sir Christopher Wren himself is just one of the many famous men interred in the crypt of St Paul's, and some, like the Duke of Wellington and Admiral Lord Nelson, are commemorated by memorials in the cathedral.

The young people of London have, since the mid nineteen-sixties, prided themselves on setting the trends, not following them. In the provinces the trio pictured *left* would certainly raise some eyebrows. Not so in London: the three elderly ladies *below* wouldn't bat an eyelid – they've seen it all before!

Far right Capturing the mood and look of the moment is a street artist in Piccadilly Circus.

London can be a maze, but the visitor who loses himself will find a veritable mine of information and assistance in the cheerful news vendor, the ever-dependable policeman or the smiling bus conductress. True Londoners are easily recognised; they have a certain indomitable spirit; an air of tolerance and reserve; a gruff kindliness. They accept life calmly and in an understated way, as they did when the Blitz raged around them. The population shifts ceaselessly, yet the character remains constant.

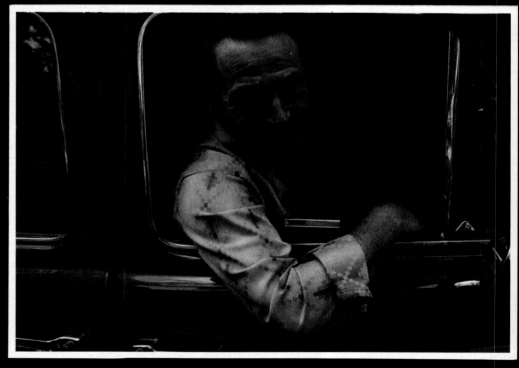

Getting around London can be a time-consuming, frustrating business. For those in a hurry, there is always the tube; for those with limitless resources a taxi cab is a comfortable and rather glamorous way to sight-see. And for those brave enough to venture into the roaring traffic, a bicycle is certainly the cheapest way to get about. But the best way by far to see London is from the top of a bus, as advised by W E Gladstone – even on a wet, steamy day it provides a clear view of the streets of the city *facing page.*

Rain in London is quite normal – snow much less so! Lasting snow before Christmas is quite rare, but lends the traditional Christmas Tree in Trafalgar Square *above right* a particularly festive air. The Tree is given each year by the people of Norway in memory of the hospitality shown to their Royal Family during the Second World War. *Facing page* Traffic grinds to a halt in the blizzard conditions.

Billingsgate, recently re-sited at East India Docks, has been the official City of London fish market since it was granted a charter in 1699. The porters, renowned for their colourful invective, wear leather hats called billy-cocks, with wide brims and flat tops, which enable them to carry up to a hundredweight of fish on their heads. The hats themselves weigh around five pounds and are handed down from father to son. The market handles an average of three hundred tons of fish every morning.

Smithfield Meat Market is the largest in the world, standing on a site covering ten acres. Designed and built by the man who rebuilt Billingsgate in 1876, Sir Horace Jones, Smithfield occupies an area of London that has housed a market since the 12th century. The area of Smithfield was once used for jousting tournaments, probably because it reflected its

derivation, Smooth Field. It was also the scene of public executions – Mary Tudor, or Bloody Mary as she was known, did away with nearly three hundred Protestants here during the Reformation.

To catch the atmosphere of Smithfield, you have to be an early riser – the busiest period is between 5.00 am and 9.00 am.

The section of Smithfield which houses poultry was rebuilt in 1962 after being destroyed by fire. Other sections in the market handle provisions, fruit and fish, but fresh and frozen meat is still the most important commodity.

The porters' down-to-earth, salty humour is common to all the London market workers, yet they look the most fearsome in their bloodstained overalls as they hump great carcases around. Smithfield is certainly the place to visit if you are toying with the idea of becoming a vegetarian!

The influx of immigrants and visitors from all over the world, together with an increase in travel and holidays abroad, has resulted in an increasing variety of foods offered in both restaurants and shops. These days it is quite common to see okra and aubergines on sale alongside cauliflowers and tomatoes in the colourful street markets. The amount of time you have available may be the only factor which decides you between opting for a full-blown meal in a French or Indian restaurant and a quick kebab, or even a traditional dish of jellied eels bought from a streetside stall. Speciality food shops abound in Soho and London's Chinatown, where herbs and spices from all over the world are freely available.

Magnificent buildings, monuments and
memorials dominate London, but it is the
population, nearly eight million in number,
that provides the city's indefinable atmosphere
and colour. The Pearlies *facing page* originated
in the late 19th century, as a revolt against
poverty and the drabness of Cockney life at
that time. Their name comes from the habit of
sewing pearl buttons onto their clothes. They
represent individual communities at various
functions and outings and their novel
appearance makes them highly successful

The Chamber of the House of Commons *right* was rebuilt and reopened in 1950 after being completely destroyed by fire during an air raid in 1941. The room is impressive, with its oak-panelled walls and green hide benches, and it is furnished with many gifts from members of the Commonwealth. To keep the governing party and its opposition a decent distance apart (traditionally two swords' length) are two red lines which members must not cross while in debate. A controversial move several years ago, to broadcast proceedings at the House of Commons, enabled the listening public to hear Parliament in session; alternatively, limited seating is available in the Public Gallery when the House is sitting.

The chapel of St Stephen's at Westminster was one of the many buildings making up the Palace of Westminster which were totally destroyed by fire in 1834. However, its crypt, built in the 13th century, still survives today. The crypt chapel *above* was used at first by courtiers while their kings worshipped in St Stephen's above them – now it serves as a place of worship for members of both the House of Lords and the House of Commons. The beautifully carved and ornate bosses depict the martyrdom of St Stephen and other saints.

The fire of 1834 gave Parliament an ideal opportunity to redesign Westminster, starting from scratch, and Sir Charles Barry was selected as architect for the new building. The House of Lords opened in 1847 and the House of Commons in 1852. Although Charles Barry conceived and designed the building, we owe its beauty to Augustus Pugin, his assistant. It is his touch that we remember when we think of the Houses of Parliament, and his eye for magnificent detail is illustrated here: *facing page* Central Lobby; *top left* Robing Room; *above* Royal Staircase; *far left* Northern Arch, Central Lobby; *left* St Stephen's Hall.

The Sovereign's Robing Room leads into the exquisitely-decorated and ornate Royal Gallery *left,* in which are two enormous frescoes: the Death of Nelson and the Meeting of Wellington and Blücher. The walls are hung with royal portraits and the gallery also contains a fascinating model of Westminster Palace at the time of Henry VIII. The floor is an intricate pattern of Minton tiles.
The Princes' Chamber *above* lies beyond, as an ante-room to the House of Lords. This sedate oak-panelled room contains a marble statue of Queen Victoria seated between Justice and Mercy, on either side of which are doors leading to the House of Lords. The walls are lined with pictures of the Tudor monarchs, below which are twelve bronze bas-reliefs depicting events which happened during their reigns. It is through the Royal Gallery and Princes' Chamber that the Queen passes on her way to open Parliament each November.

London is a virtual treasure-trove for those interested in the fine arts. Mayfair has a wonderful selection of art galleries and rare book shops while Charing Cross Road is lined with small, dusty but fascinating establishments selling second-hand books. Near the British Museum, in Great Russell

Street, is Robert Douwma *above*, one of numerous print and map shops to be found in the city.
Millions of pounds change hands every year at the world-famous Sotheby's auction-rooms *facing page*. Founded in 1744, Sotheby's originally specialised in rare books and manuscripts, but have now turned their attention to art, becoming the world's leading art auctioneers. It is really exhilarating watching a sale – the average speed is two lots per minute!

The skyline of London has changed considerably over the years since World War II, and St Paul's, which once dominated it, is now almost dwarfed by the glass and steel skyscrapers which are rising up around the city. These aerial photographs, taken on a slightly hazy summer's day, illustrate the jumble of buildings surrounding the Cathedral, and it is easy to pick out that other great landmark, the Post Office Tower, on the skyline *above*.

St James's Park and Green Park provide welcome greenery amid the grandeur of Whitehall and The Mall *right,* at the far end of which is situated Buckingham Palace. Green Park provides a link between St James's and Hyde Park and is the smallest of all the royal parks. *Above* The Thames flows past Millbank Tower and under Lambeth and Westminster Bridges, curving at Hungerford railway bridge before reaching Waterloo Bridge. Although many road and rail bridges now cross The Thames, it was over sixteen hundred years before a second bridge was built across the river after the Romans put up the first one to Southwark.

Imaginative illumination has made the best of London's landmarks at night: Nelson stands proudly on top of his column in Trafalgar Square *left,* while *below left* the huge dome of St Paul's is highlighted against a purple evening sky. Ornate lamps twinkle against the severe backdrop of the Law Courts *below*; a much gayer scene is Theatreland – Wyndhams, Ambassadors and St Martin's are just three of the famous theatres to be found in London's West End.

Christmas decorations brighten the windows of Oxford Street for those last-minute shoppers, *facing page*

Paddington Station *facing page* **is one of the most important of the fifteen chief railway termini that serve London, connecting the capital city with the western part of the country, and it was between Paddington and Bristol that the high-speed Intercity 125 made its first scheduled run. A similar structure, but** **performing an entirely different function, is the Central Market Building, Covent Garden** *far right***, once the home of the famous fruit, flower and vegetable market which is now located on the south side of the River Thames, and now a leisure area, comprising galleries, street cafés** **and shopping arcades. The street markets of London, like Petticoat Lane and Portobello Road, are still very good for picking up bargains although, as with markets everywhere, it is advisable to look things over very carefully before you buy!**

Top left **Liverpool Street Station;** *far left* **Spitalfields Market;** *above* **the Whale Hall in the Natural History Museum;** *left* **the Stock Exchange.**
Bunting criss-crosses the already colourful streets around Petticoat Lane Market *facing page.*

Top The Royal Festival Hall, seen here in a blaze of light, was erected in 1951, and the then innovative design has proved to be highly successful. The acoustics are thought by many to be the best in the world and, together with the Royal Albert Hall, it is home of the auditorium where most of London's major concerts are played. *Above and facing page* Piccadilly Circus is one of London's best-

known landmarks and has a virtually magnetic attraction for tourists. Although undergoing substantial redevelopment, it will undoubtedly retain its famous Shaftesbury Memorial, topped by the figure of the Angel of Christian Charity – nicknamed and better-known as Eros (the God of Love). From the Circus it is just a short walk into Soho and Rathbone Place for a drink at the Wheatsheaf.

Some of the more familiar sights of London are (clockwise from top left) St Paul's Cathedral, Tower Hotel, The Monument, Covent Garden, the Bank of England and Royal Exchange, and Tower Bridge. *Facing page* A light in the Clock Tower signifies another late night session for the House of Commons.

London is not just concrete and glass and traffic fumes – trees and greenery can be found in the most unlikely of places, and they provide an oasis both for the tourist and the Londoner. What better way to relax than a trip on Regent's Canal *far left*, or an hour or two by the bandstand in St James's Park *far left below*? Watching the river flow by at Cadogan Pier, Chelsea, can be equally pleasurable *below*. Or a walk around some of the delightful mews cottages in Hampstead *left*. And to round

it off, a drink and lunch in the garden of one of the many excellent pubs that London is famous for – like The Old Bull and Bush *left*, between Hampstead and Golders Green, or The Flask *right*, Highgate, where Dick Turpin and later William Hogarth once drank.

Scenes like these are familiar in the city's pubs, where young and old meet for a drink after work perhaps, a good chat, or a sing-song. The establishments themselves can range from large and plush to tiny and cramped; they can be cosy and comfortable, or 'spit-and-sawdust', but every pub has its regulars. Pubs are wonderful places for celebrations, particularly royal celebrations, when flags and bunting festoon the bar area.

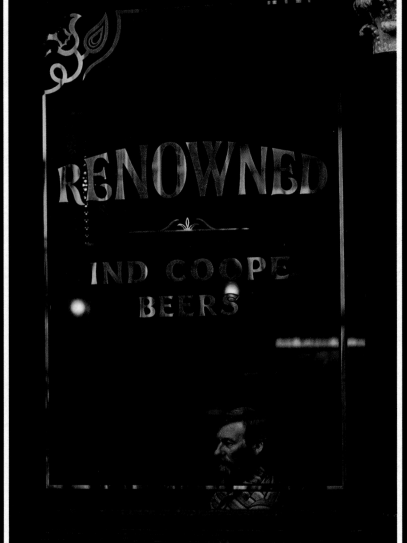

As Dr Samuel Johnson said: 'There is nothing which has been contrived by man by which so much happiness is produced as by a good tavern or inn.' Certainly the customers of these establishments would agree with him. Wine bars are becoming increasingly popular, offering interesting food with a good selection of wines by the glass or bottle. To the visitor to this country, and indeed to many of its residents, our licensing laws are archaic – the hours when alcoholic liquor can be sold differ throughout Britain, but in London they are generally between 11.00 am and 3.00 pm, and 5.30 pm and 11.00 pm. Sunday hours are normally from 12.00 to 2.00 pm and from 7.00 pm to 10.30 pm.

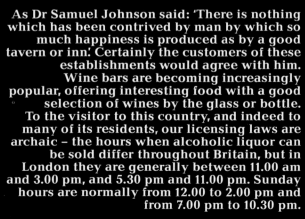

The silhouette of the Clock Tower and Houses of Parliament must be one of the most distinctive in the world. Black against a blood-red sky, it looms above a glistening River Thames *right,* while *above,* and seen from the opposite direction, its spires pierce the purple evening.

Buckingham Palace, the London home of the Queen, is a main attraction for tourists at all times of the year. The ceremony of Changing the Guard takes place there daily and the splash of colour it provides never fails to draw an audience.

Annual ceremonial occasions, such as Trooping the Colour in June, bring the spectacle of divisions of the Household Brigades, with their brilliant scarlet and black uniforms, shining helmets and breastplates and beautifully groomed horses. Now and again, in the splendour of a Jubilee or Royal Wedding, the whole panoply of military brilliance is brought into action with that legendary precision which makes such occasions truly and unmistakably British.

Individual Guards regiments can be identified by the pattern of button-spacing on their uniform – the Guards *right* and *above* are Welsh, while *far right* it is the Coldstream Guards who troop their colour.

are major attractions for the visitor to Royal London – yet the Londoner himself takes these displays very much for granted. *Left* The Royal Horse Artillery fires a 41-gun salute in honour of the Queen's Birthday – 21 for royalty and 20 to honour the city of London. The salute takes place in Hyde Park. Evoking days gone by, a horse-drawn carriage makes its way along Rotten Row *right*. The military band *below* contains

members of several Guard's regiments, individual regiments being distinguished not only by the spacing of the buttons on their coats, but by the coloured plumes on their bearskins: the Grenadiers have a white plume on the left of the bearskin, the Coldstreams have a scarlet plume on the right, the Irish a pale blue plume on the right, and the Welsh a white and green plume on the left. The Scots Guards are plumeless'!

The magnificent interior of Armourers' and Brasiers' Hall *left*, first built in the 15th century and rebuilt in 1840, makes a truly memorable setting for a formal lunch or dinner.

Of colourful appearance themselves, and a familiar sight in the King's Road area, are pensioners from the Royal Hospital, Chelsea. The hospital was founded in 1682 by Charles II and provides a permanent home for veteran soldiers of 'good character.'

Floodlit monuments and memorials line the
streets and river banks, their stark lines
softened and detail highlighted: the
Renaissance-style GLC Building – County Hall
– dominates the south bank *above;* further
along the river on the north bank, and adjacent
to Waterloo Bridge is Somerset House *top left.*
A total contrast of style is seen in Gothic
Westminster Abbey *remaining pictures.*

Standing guard over the river approaches to
the city is the mighty White Tower, fortress of
William the Conqueror, seen *facing page* from
the south bank of the river. The Tower of
London was a chilling sight for those entering
it by way of Traitor's Gate. Elizabeth I was one
of the few who entered the Tower this way and
survived.

Wet pavements reflect the lights of Parliament Square. The Square, its grass centre surrounded by statues of great men, was the first site of the roundabout system back in 1926, and the constant flow of traffic around it now makes it occasionally quite difficult for pedestrians to reach!

The brooding figure, by Ivor Roberts-Jones, of Sir Winston Churchill faces the House of Commons, while an almost jaunty statue of Field-Marshal Smuts, by Sir Jacob Epstein, looks out over the Square and beyond.

Facing page A colourful display in Harrod's Food Hall.

The lights of London shimmer against a black, rain-sodden sky, as weary commuters make their way home.

The parks have been called the 'lungs of London' and they certainly provide breathing space for Londoners and tourists alike. Under the canopy of Hyde Park's delightful bandstand, a military band plays for a handful of listeners *left* – traditional summer entertainment. The appearance of the sun (all too infrequent in Britain) brings out the crowds to stroll around the Serpentine, play football, feed the ducks, or just sit around on the grass. *Right* Pale pink blossom on a flowering cherry tree in St James's Park heralds the approach of summer and the end of a long, harsh winter.

Scenes from a London summer – straw-boatered schoolgirls, the Heath at Hampstead *top right*, and cricket at Battersea. The superb aerial view of Hampton Court Palace *right* shows parts of the formal gardens to their best advantage. Given to Henry VIII by Cardinal Wolsey, the Palace is so steeped in atmosphere that one almost expects to see Henry and one of his wives strolling through the grounds.

Pigeons circle Nelson's Column, sharing their airspace over Trafalgar Square with a 'blimp' *above,* **while geese, swans and ducks join the evening rowers on a glinting Serpentine** *right.*

The somewhat inappropriately-named Egyptian Hall *left* at Mansion House is laid for lunch for the incoming and outgoing Lord Mayors after the annual election on Michaelmas Day.

Cardinal Cap Alley, on the south side of the river, is an excellent vantage point for St Paul's Cathedral *above* and *facing page*, and indeed Sir Christopher Wren himself was able to watch the progress of construction from his home adjoining the alley.

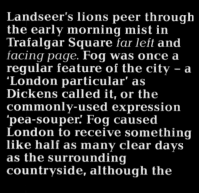

Landseer's lions peer through the early morning mist in Trafalgar Square *far left* and *facing page.* Fog was once a regular feature of the city – a 'London particular' as Dickens called it, or the commonly-used expression 'pea-souper.' Fog caused London to receive something like half as many clear days as the surrounding countryside, although the

incidence of this happening has decreased considerably since the introduction of anti-pollution laws and smokeless zones.

The mist creates an eerie atmosphere, out of which ghostly statues, memorials and monuments loom menacingly.

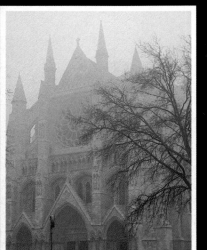

Dawn breaks over London, the Thames shimmers and the quiet streets glow in the weak sunlight. A bronze griffin *left* marks Temple Bar and the City boundary, replacing a gate which, until 1745, displayed the heads of the executed! It is here that, on State occasions, the Monarch requests permission of the Lord Mayor to enter the city.

Historic Guildhall, the seat of government of the City, is pictured *above* and *left;* the extraordinary view of London and the Thames *right* was taken from the tallest building in London, the National Westminster Tower.

The life-giving sun rises and sets over a river that gave London life – the ever-winding, ancient Thames.

The vast sprawl of London has, over the years, swallowed up large numbers of villages and hamlets, yet many retain their individual character. Greenwich was a mediaeval fishing village until it caught the eye of the Tudors, who decided to hold court there. The Queen's House is shown in the centre of the photograph *right*. Built for Anne of Denmark and, upon her death, for Henrietta Maria, wife of Charles I, it is linked by colonnades to the National Maritime Museum. Up river lies another village with royal connections; Richmond *left* and *top left*. Strand-on-the-Green *remaining photographs*, near Kew, remains a delightfully pretty riverside hamlet, but despite its name, it boasts no green at all!

One of the best ways to see London is from its river, and pleasure boats cruise up and down regularly during the tourist season. Yet the Thames is essentially a working river, flanked by jetties, docks and wharves as well as numerous historic buildings.

As tranquil as a mill-pond, the Thames has a wonderfully reflective quality, transforming stark detail and harsh outline into soft iridescent images. The London skies have attracted many painters, each trying to capture the rapidly changing cloud formations and hues, seemingly peculiar to this great city. The long sunsets are a special feature, the skies turning deep saffron or vivid violet.

The old blends with the new as contemporary tower blocks soar above the old Roman city wall *top left.* Parts of the wall, built at the end of the 2nd century AD, can be seen between the huge office blocks of the innovative and exciting Barbican development *below left,* which houses flats, shops, offices and a recently completed ultra-modern theatre and concert-hall complex. *Top right* The tallest building in the country, the National Westminster tower, at 600 feet high and with 52 floors, dwarfs even the giants of the Barbican.

Lights strung like pearls adorn the South Bank, with its pleasant walkways and magnificent views *facing page.*

Masts, spires, towers and domes crowd the skyline of London: *top left* the rigging of the Cutty Sark, in dry dock at Greenwich, creates a delicate pattern against the sky. The intricate Albert Memorial *top right* was once described as 'the finest monumental structure in Europe'. Pictured *far left below* is the lighthouse-like Post Office Tower; the lightship Nore

lies in St Katherine's Dock *below centre. Above* The famous symbol of justice crowns a domed Old Bailey.

A tremendous curve in the course of the Thames creates the illusion that St Paul's has moved across the river to the south side *facing page*. The splendid GLC building dominates the foreground.

The twin towers on the West Front of
Westminster Abbey *below* were added in the
18th century. Built of Portland stone, they look
most impressive when seen from a distance;
otherwise they are dwarfed by the immense
hulk of the Abbey itself. *Right* Feathery spray
shimmers in the lights of the Christmas Tree on
Trafalgar Square.

Scarlet leather and gilt dominate the House of
Lords *facing page.* Above the Sovereign's throne
is a highly carved canopy, its ornamentation
contrasting strongly with the simple
Woolsack, the seat of the Lord Chancellor,
situated directly in front of the throne. The
Woolsack has been, since the time of
Edward III, a reminder of the days when
England's wealth relied upon its wool trade.

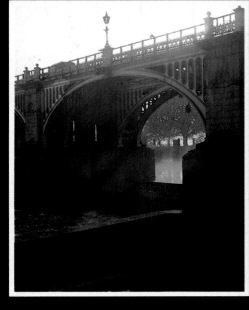

Sunrise brings a delicate mist; it hangs like gossamer over the river and through it the Victorian footbridge at Richmond seems suspended in mid-air. Shadowy figures make their way through the utter stillness of Old Deer Park *above* while in nearby Richmond Park, created by Charles I, a magnificent stag is camouflaged against the foliage. The deer that roam Richmond Park can be very friendly but are extremely unpredictable and should not be approached.

There is so much to see and do in London that the visitor really needs to spend at least a full month here to gain anything more than a superficial impression. Pictured on these pages are a variety of attractions: *above right* Westminster Abbey (from the Dean's Yard); *facing page* the White Tower, Tower of London; *right* daffodils in Hyde Park, and *far right* a charming street in Old Windsor.

The unmistakable Clock Tower at the north end of the Houses of Parliament is commonly described as 'Big Ben,' but in fact the name 'Big Ben' applies to the huge bronze hour-bell inside the Tower, seen here *facing page.* Named after Sir Benjamin Hall, first Commissioner of Works, the bell weighs over 13½ tons and was cast at Whitechapel in 1858. The clock itself has four dials, each 23 feet in diameter. The figures are 2 feet high and the hands are 9 feet and 14 feet long. Part of the mechanism is shown *below;* the pendulum which is responsible for the perfect time-keeping is over twice the height of a man and beats once every two seconds.

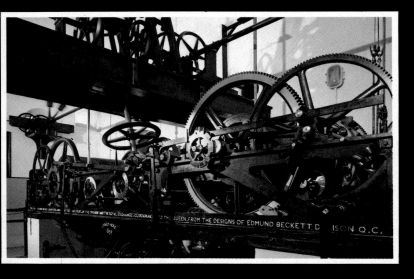

Lovely St James's Park, seen *above* **in warm spring sunshine, became, and still is, one of the most popular walks in London, although it certainly was not for Charles I – for it was through the Park from St James's Palace to Horse Guards that he took his final steps to the scaffold! The Park was remodelled in 1829 by John Nash who created the enchanting lake, a favourite haunt for waterfowl and the famous pelicans. The elegant façade of Buckingham Palace is reflected in its rippling waters. Tower Bridge** *right* **takes on a dream-like, Turneresque quality in the pink light of dawn.**

London has always been famed for its parks and open spaces, its statues, memorials and great houses. The ornamental gates *bottom* lead into Queen Mary's Garden, Regents Park and *bottom right* is the Victoria and Albert Memorial, seen over a sea of daffodils. Hyde Park in April is shown *right,* and *below* is Kenwood House, Hampstead. Deer still roam the open spaces of Richmond Park *left.*

In these days of mass-production, it is still possible to buy made-to-measure goods of the finest quality. James Lock & Co *left* and *below* are the most distinguished hatters in the world, while John Lobb *bottom left and right* supplies superior hand-made shoes. Wine merchants Berry Brothers & Rudd occupy an 18th century building full of fine wines and atmosphere *facing page.*

The splendid interior of the Guildhall *right* has
been the scene of many important events –
traitors were condemned here, Lord Mayors
have held their banquets and receptions for
visiting Kings, Emperors and Presidents here,
and it is at Guildhall that the Freedom of the
City is conferred on heroes, patriots and
statesmen. Its two most famous residents are
Gog *below right* and Magog *below left,* these
wooden giants representing the struggle
between ancient Britons and the Trojans.
Apothecaries' Hall *bottom* dates back to the
17th century. The society is an examining body
in surgery and medicine.

Facing page **London by night, its bridges
crossing the mighty Thames.**